Author:
Imani Jean

Illustrator:
Zebulun Dinkins

I0541696

Imani's Voice, Imani's Victory:
The Road to a National Championship

Published by: Hayward Jean, Speak Life Publishing
Illustrations by: Zebulun Dinkins, ME Animations
Book Graphics, Layout & Design: Starlette Jean
Editors: Starlette Jean, Dorthy Richberg, and Hayward Jean

ISBN: 979-8-9856055-1-8
Library of Congress Control Number: 2025933207

Printed in the United States of America

Thank you God, for loving me. Thank you for protecting me and helping me to inspire others through speaking and sharing my story. Thank you for shining your light through me. I love you God.

To every little boy and girl who has ever faced challenges on the way to victory, this book is dedicated to you.
No matter your challenge, I hope my book inspires you to keep going for your dreams.

To my brothers, Micah and Malachi, thank you for encouraging me. During my tough times, you would come into my room and build me back up. Thank you for always having my back.
I love you so much boys.

To Daddy and Mommy, thank you for pulling out my gifts and talents. You push me to do my best. Even when I think I cannot go any further, you help me to believe in myself.
Daddy and Mommy, I love you.

Meet **Imani**, a bright and happy little girl with big dreams.

When she was younger, her dad and mom loved sharing cool, funny stories about her, and everyone laughed. *ha ha ha*

Imani **loved** to sing on her brother's karaoke machine. She would sing and dance around the house.

She also loved reciting her favorite Bible verses and encouraging her teachers while she was in school.

Imani admired her dad, who was a great speaker. When she was younger, she copied him, and her mom compared them to a famous boxing daddy-daughter duo, jokingly calling them the "Muhammad and Laila Ali" of speaking.

Whenever anyone asked Imani what she wanted to be when she grew up, she always said, "A teacher and a speaker, just like my daddy!"

Imani loved school. She played with her friends and learned exciting new things. Her teachers often picked her for opportunities to represent her class in different school programs and ceremonies.

Imani's school counselor asked her to give the farewell speech at the end-of-year ceremony for her second-grade class. SO COOL!

After the speech, people celebrated her and praised her courage for speaking in front of so many people with such passion.

Imani entered a new school, and although she was nervous, she quickly made new friends. Yay!

She joined a unique program all about broadcasting and journalism. Imani learned about studios, how to record interviews, how to produce shows, and went on many field trips to different news stations.

Imani's teachers allowed her to be the Broadcasting Studio Manager. She was so excited!

THIS WAS AMAZING!

In her new adventure, Imani would shine with dreams in her heart of becoming a news anchor.

One day, her teacher announced it was time for the annual Dr. Martin Luther King Jr. (MLK) Oratory Competition. "Raise your hand if you want to participate in the MLK Oratory Competition," she said. Some students started **BUZZING** with excitement!

Knowing what the competition was all about, Imani's heart raced as she raised her hand. Her friends, who knew how much she loved speaking, started yelling, "Yeah, Imani! You should do it!"

The competition was a big deal. Imani felt ready and nervous all at the same time.

Imani won her class competition, which earned her a spot in the school-level competition. But just a couple of days before the event, the unexpected happened: Imani got sick. **UGH!**

Her mom said, "It's okay, Imani. You'll still have another chance next year. Let's focus on you getting better." There was just one problem: Imani didn't want to wait. **Yikes!**

"I can do it, Mommy! I've got this!" said Imani. Her mom kept asking, "Are you sure?" Imani nodded and replied, "**YES**, I'm sure!" Imani's dad agreed, saying, "She's good; let her do it."

So, Imani and her mom practiced hard every day to prepare for the competition.

FINALLY, the moment arrived. A call from the hallway shouted: "Imani, it's your turn!" Her heart pounded fast as she walked into the cafeteria to take the stage. Not feeling her best, she took a deep breath, whispered a prayer and then gave it her all.

After all the speeches, everyone returned to the stage for the big announcement. "Congratulations, Imani, you are on your way to the District MLK Oratory Competition!" said the announcer. Imani couldn't believe it;

She won!

Imani was now ready for the next level of competition. She was hyped and ready to represent her school. Little did Imani know, she was preparing for more than one challenge.

Many people didn't realize that Imani was practicing and memorizing several speeches at the same time.

It was a big challenge for a little girl, but she kept saying to herself, "I got this. **I'M GOOD.** I better make sure I don't confuse my speeches," with a playful grin.

While preparing for the District MLK Oratory Competition, she also prepared for and won the South Carolina Beta Club Speech Competition in the same month.

This win qualified Imani for the National Junior Beta Club Speech Competition, which would take place later in the summer. Imani was ready to take on the world, **one speech at a time!**

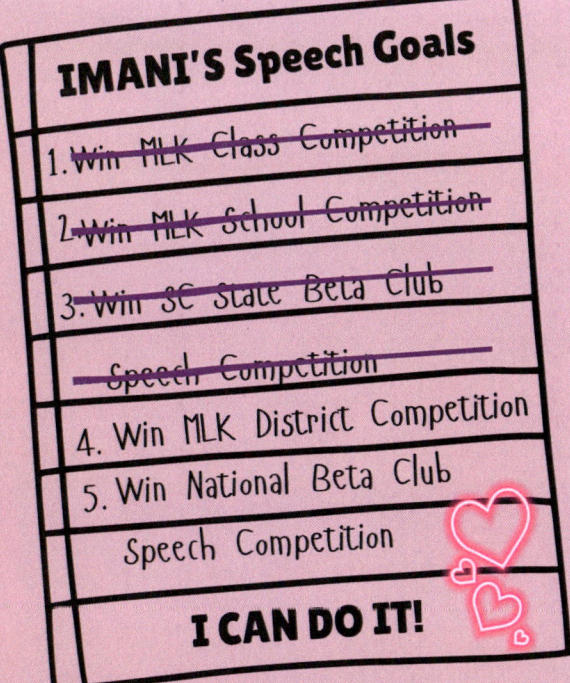

IMANI'S Speech Goals

1. ~~Win MLK Class Competition~~
2. ~~Win MLK School Competition~~
3. ~~Win SC State Beta Club~~
   ~~Speech Competition~~
4. Win MLK District Competition
5. Win National Beta Club
   Speech Competition

I CAN DO IT!

Imani spent lots of time with the other school winners of the District MLK Oratory Competition, making new friends and practicing her big speech with her coach.

The other contestants would laugh and tell silly jokes while practicing fun ways to cheer for each other during the trophy presentation.

It was time for the big night. Imani and the other contestants were ready to showcase their hard work.

It was Imani's turn. **Whew!**

With her heart **POUNDING** again, she went on stage to deliver a passionate speech! The words flowed like a beautiful song. After the speech, Imani felt happy and proud of what she had done, no matter the outcome.

She couldn't wait to share this unforgettable night of joy with her friends and family.

One by one, the names of the contestants were called, and Imani felt her heart beating faster and faster. Finally, the announcer said her name as the

1st Place Winner!

Imani couldn't believe it; she was the new District MLK Oratory Competition winner! The moment she DREAMED of and worked hard for was finally here!

Standing in shock, she smiled as she looked out into the crowd. Her friends were jumping and cheering with all their hearts, and some of her teachers and family were there too, clapping and celebrating her!

Imani's Beta Club advisor smiled and said, "**CONGRATULATIONS**, we want to do this same thing at Nationals!"

Imani felt so happy and proud, knowing her hard work paid off. She knew this was just the beginning of even more celebrations.

Imani felt like a true champion. But when she stepped off the stage, something surprised her.

She noticed that not everyone seemed excited for her. Even the people she loved (and thought loved her) were not so friendly. This made Imani feel confused and sad.

She wondered why people were upset with her victory.

On the ride home, instead of celebrating, Imani asked her mom, "Mommy, do people think I cheated?"

Her mom looked surprised and said,

"Imani," her mom said with tears in her eyes, "you worked very hard and deserve to win just like anyone else! Now is not the time to worry about what others think."

That night, Imani's family felt a lot of emotions seeing her down during such a happy time.

It wasn't exactly the way they thought the night would happen, but her parents and brothers worked together to make her feel special.

They reminded her how proud they were, and to help Imani focus on the joy, they celebrated with pizza—one of her favorite foods! Yummy!

Imani returned to school as a winner, struggling to enjoy her victory. No matter how she felt, Imani's family and friends would not allow people's negative thoughts and comments to stop her from reaching her dream of being a speaker.

Imani was determined to keep practicing and working hard for her next big competition.

Imani's dad cheered for his superstar speaker as she practiced every day. "Imani, you were born for this!" he said. "Keep working hard for nationals, and win again! You have to be ready!"

Her big brother would echo, "That's right, Imani. Let's GOOO! Do it again. WIN!"
Their words motivated Imani every day as she practiced for the next big speech.

Finally, the moment Imani had been waiting for arrived. She and her friends loaded the bus for the National Junior Beta Club Convention. The ride to the convention was so much fun!

On competition day, Imani was a little nervous because she would be competing against over 30 other students from 19 different states. WHOA! Imani knew she could shine bright on that stage!

She had won before, so why not go for the win again? She prayed to God and was ready to do her best.

After delivering her speech, "A Voyage of Adventure," Imani and the other contestants eagerly awaited the results. When the results were posted, Imani and her school's club members jumped up with joy! Imani had made it into the top 5!

On a big stage filled with bright lights and a beautiful background designed for superstars, the announcer said, "And your 2024 National Beta Club Speech Champion is...Imani Jean from Edisto Elementary School!"

yaaaayyyyyyyyy!!!

The crowd went wild! Everyone cheered and hollered. Tears of happiness filled Imani's eyes, along with a tight-lipped smile, as she walked off the stage, surrounded by friends who were screaming with excitement. They hugged her and twirled her around.

Imani's dad greeted her with the biggest hug and a kiss. Her brothers looked at her in amazement, mouths wide open, clapping, while her mom hugged her tightly, with tears in her eyes. "You did it, Imani! You did it!" she said.

Imani was now a **National Champion!**

Leaving the convention center, Imani turned to her mom, "Mommy, I did it! I'm a National Champion!"

"Thank you, Lord!" Imani exclaimed, thanking God for the courage and strength. Her joy warmed her family's hearts. "You deserve it! This is just the beginning. There is so much more for you to do. Keep dreaming and speaking!" her parents said.

Imani returned home feeling happy and excited about all the adventures awaiting her. She confidently danced around the house, holding her trophy and singing, "I'm a National Champion!" "Yes, you are!" her dad and mom replied.

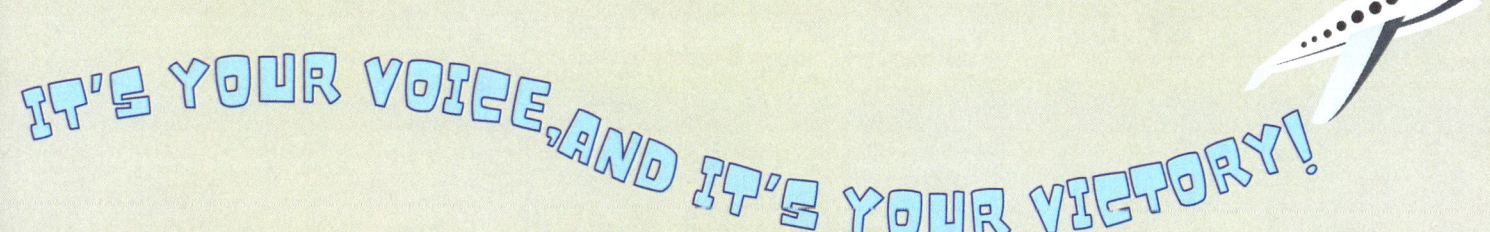

IT'S YOUR VOICE, AND IT'S YOUR VICTORY!

ABOUT THE AUTHOR

Imani Jean is a 5th-grade scholar in Orangeburg County School District. She is the daughter of Mr. and Mrs. Hayward and Starlette Jean, and the youngest of three, including her big brothers, Micah and Malachi.

As an academic scholar, Imani is an honor roll student, manager of her school's Broadcasting and Journalism Academy (BAJA), school ambassador, and is identified by the State Department of Education as a Gifted & Talented student.

Imani has a passion for empowering people through uplifting messages, both in person and on social media.

She has won multiple speech contests at the local, state, and national levels.

Imani has a YouTube channel entitled
Imani Inspires,
which is also the name of her speaking platform.

She aspires to launch a girls' empowerment conference. She also enjoys spending time with her family, traveling, singing, laughing, playing games, and playing volleyball.

Imani wants to attend Claflin University to become a mass communications professional. Her favorite quote is, "Don't just have a dream, but be the dream!"

Meet Imani's Family

Beta Club National Convention
Savannah, GA

CONNECT WITH THE AUTHOR

Did this story inspire you?

 bethedreamimani@gmail.com

 haywardjean.com

 Imani Inspires
@imaniinspires2013

 imani.inspires

DON' JUST HAVE THE DREAM BE THE DREAM

Imani
ASPIRES

YOUR VOICE
YOUR VICTORY

www.ingramcontent.com/pod-product-compliance
Lightning Source LLC
Chambersburg PA
CBRC090839120626
46551CB00008B/706